ACHE

JOSEPH ROSS

SIBLING RIVALRY PRESS
LITTLE ROCK, ARKANSAS
DISTURB / ENRAPTURE

Sibling Rivalry Press, LLC
PO Box 26147
Little Rock, AR 72221

info@siblingrivalrypress.com

www.siblingrivalrypress.com

ISBN: 978-1-943977-31-4

Library of Congress Control No: 2016959042

This title is housed permanently in the Rare Books and Special
Collections Vault of the Library of Congress.

First Sibling Rivalry Press Edition, March 2017

For Robert

Poets who write mostly about love, roses and moonlight, sunsets and snow, must lead a very quiet life.

Langston Hughes
from his essay,
"My Life as a Social Poet"
Good Morning Revolution

Meeting

---

for Robert

We weren't supposed to
meet that night. But the

June evening air was ready
to speak. Friends

laughed around us
in their own language.

We spoke in words
and sipped the water

beneath the words.
I told you my father's name;

you whispered yours.
Our mothers were already

conspiring in our mutual joy.
The wooden walls of that

dining room baptized us
with quiet longing.

You wrote your number
on a green paper napkin

that found its way to my
skin. I held it close,

between my fingers
and my chest. I still hold it

there. I saw kindness
at the edges of your eyes. I felt

a trembling at the edges
of my breath, as if someone

were playing a cello in the
distance. As if I had forgotten

the song's name but not
its ache.

Coltrane's Breath

The air escapes
Coltrane's lips,

swelling through the sky
of his alto sax.

His blood cascades
down his arms, loving

his hands, home to his
fingertips, pooling, waiting

to touch the keys
like swollen skin.

His breath hides
in the saxophone's

bow until the finger tip
begs the key open

for that one gasp
of escape, a swirl

around the instrument's
bell and out

into the aching world.

On John Coltrane's "Alabama"

9/15/1963
*Remembering Addie Mae Collins, Denise McNair,
Carole Robertson, and Cynthia Wesley*

There are no words
for brick dust or fallen beams.

Only a piano rumbling,
a ceiling collapsing.

There is no sky in September
when a stand-up bass

has to preach
forgiveness, when an

angry man drives
away from a church smiling.

Cymbals wince in shock,
stunned at the space

between drum beats,
pauses in a preacher's cadence

that convert no one.
Drums only sing in one

language but the maker
of this Confederate memory

does not recognize this
tongue. Pressing breath

into a saxophone cannot
resuscitate polished Sunday

shoes, a blue satin dress,
a dead girl's hand pointing

to a window.

On John Coltrane's "A Love Supreme"

1. Acknowledgment

If Emily Dickinson's poems
echo the four-line verses
of New England hymnals:

symmetrical praise
of an asymmetrical God—
the four notes of this praise

live in the symmetry of air;
they come from the sanctuary
of the lung, a dark, moist mass

of human breath.
This breath chants out four
flames of praise,

the bass pulses four exultations,
the cymbals wash over it
in a baptismal litany,

a statement of what is:
a man exhales the love
from which he is made.

That love sang supreme
and lived among us.

2. Resolution

A Ugandan boy runs
barefoot on a dirt path,
brown as his skin,

packed hard as the martyrs'
dried blood. His feet push
the earth with questions.

He learns that uncertainty
always lives in dust. His wet
lungs constrict and enlarge, his

face bleeds water, his lips
stretch, imagining the lush
of his destination, the answers,
only lament can teach.

3. Pursuance

The gazelle does not know
the lion watches, exhaling.
But the ground beneath

the ground does. The unknowing
seems natural enough until
its symmetries burst in

four directions, arcing
across the sky, leaving
a smoldering burn

behind them. We wail.
It is the language
inside every tongue.

Human wailing sounds like
death but it's actually
a boy looking at himself

in the water and seeing
no moon, no sun, no self,
only a shining.

4. Psalm

The shining lives just
beneath the other darkness.
It waits in its own smiling

sky about to thunder with
elation, about to rip open
a swollen cloud and wash

every wound under
every other wound. It can't
contain anything. It can hold

everything: our broken bones,
our forgotten names, a boy
with arms like a river,

yearning to praise.

On John Coltrane's "Lush Life"

There are no saxophones
in the desert.

No saguaro has
the necessary delicacy.

Its needles cannot fold
and press like skin.

Its cactus flesh too
firm and rigid.

A saxophone needs
supple, lush. When human

breath swims through its
golden canyons it sings

only if the player bends.
Humans too require

moistness, a waterfall
of possible,

a baptism in bending.
Wanderers survive only

when the desert trails
are lush enough for one

note, soaring skyward,
dressed in glistening

restraint.

On John Coltrane's "After the Rain"

Even the air seems
to take a breath

once the shower gives
way to a dry mercy.

The watery saxophone
and the piano's chilly

glance speak the language
of relief, of danger

averted. They tell us
in dialogue, one speaking

respectfully after
the other that we can

sleep knowing,
we can breathe out

gladness. The world
circles a sun.

The clouds are not
still. They too whisper

to their lover in the dark
even after he is

asleep.

On John Coltrane & Duke Ellington's
"In a Sentimental Mood"

When a piano stacks river
stones, smooth as tears

on your lover's back.
When a saxophone turns

like your first bike, golden
and leaning toward trust.

When a stand-up bass
whispers in the language

of scars with names.
When a drum tightens

like skin under the brush
of a human finger that stays

a second longer than you
expect it to. Here lives

the pulse, that human
threat to order, the rebel

armed with a tongue,
unafraid to trace another's

living skin.

On John Coltrane's "Reverend King"

The tenor sax sings the concrete
of Auburn Avenue, grand-parents,
front porch. It whispers

Morehouse and tries to read
music it hasn't learned yet. It gathers
into a man's voice to chant Boston.

Here, the sax weaves a love song,
falling over itself for a rhythm
that could carry it, outlive it.

It deepens and moves South to a
Montgomery of empty buses, kitchen prayers,
bombs, threatened and real. Then drums rise

to an angry Birmingham. The verses
hum jailed, their tones are letters,
grace notes, staccato police batons

slice the air like the conductors
of an insane choir. Coltrane's breath
rushes through the saxophone now.

The tune terrors in Vietnam. It prays
scared in Selma. Its notes are water hoses,
dog teeth, indifference. It sings symphony

in Washington, chaos in Chicago. 1963
was cruel to this melody, this unfinished
lunch counter where four little girls

sit side-by-side and eat
nothing. So finally he puts down the sax
as it fills with tears, unplayable. He takes

up the bass clarinet because it sounds
more like fury, like staring down a President.
This song knows harmony. It is a choir

called Watts. It sings riot in a new tongue:
the language of the un-heard. This song swirls
now, it fills the world house with a straight-

spined melody. This tune sings garbage men
who are men. This rhythm has walked
to a mountaintop. It tastes like a promise.

So it clears its throat and soars,
singing: Memphis.

◄

What do the people we call prophets know?

Martín Espada
from "Stone Hammered to Gravel"
The Republic of Poetry

Nelson Mandela, Prisoner No. 46664

Your island world
could only breathe

through one window.
A prison ringed

with stone, keeping
the ocean out, resisting

its licks and hurls.
You stand over rocks

that took centuries
to form and do not want

to crack at a moment's
hammer. This posture,

a sentence of standing
to read, to believe

every waking breath
need not be a war.

Every resting breath
need not be an ache.

Nelson Mandela Burns His Passbook, 1952

You had to carry a passbook
in your own country,

which meant, of course,
it wasn't. Except that

you refused that meaning,
it being too false to fit into

your pocket, too insulting to press
against your persistent skin.

But you were over the legal
sixteen years of age,

old enough to know just whose
country this is not.

When you burned
your passbook, you knelt down

in good shoes, a dress shirt
buttoned to the neck. You lit

the passbook and held it
above a cooking kettle.

You thought you might eat
its ashes for dinner. The blue

flame, tiny and cautious at first,
crawled up the paper like a

well-dressed thief, about to steal
what is already his.

Nelson Mandela Speaks to Hector Pieterson

Hector Pieterson, age 13, was killed on June 16, 1976
by South African police along with 176 others in the
Soweto Youth Massacre.

I sit greying in this granite country,
crushing rocks into angry gravel.

You run on a road of stones
from a language you refuse

to throw. Why are another man's
words fired at you?

Why can't you chant a psalm
of stones to shield you?

Why must you run
in our limping country?

I did not want to learn of you,
Hector Pieterson. I wanted to hold you.

I did not want to call your mother
a hero. I wanted to call her

grandmother.

Nelson Mandela Speaks to Mamie Till

On some August nights I think
every mother is a martyr.

I know you would resist that
thought. It was your son,

you would say, not you. And you
would be right. And you would be

wrong. Mothers loved sons
in 1955, especially when the sons

slept hundreds of miles away.
I was banned that year. It was

the beginning of living
in rocks, behind rocks.

By the end, I knew about walls.
You knew walls too: wooden

walls of barns, where screams
could not be seen, transparent

walls of coffins, letting a country
see what it had to save.

Nelson Mandela Speaks to Tupac Shakur

Some say we
have nothing
in common.

But we were
both born
into revolution

and lived.
We sang
the same century

though it rarely
sang to us.
We read the bad

news of ghettos
and tried to write
a gospel they could

believe. You loved
your mother like
a country.

I loved my country
like the mother
she was not.

In a city of light
you were killed
too soon.

In a country
at dawn I keep
being born.

Nelson Mandela Speaks to Trayvon Martin

I walk down Fox Street
in Johannesburg at dawn.

A light rain darkens my shoes,
they scrape against the small

stones. I am standing
in the doorway when I see you

across the street, on the corner,
looking at me. You wear no hood

today. You smile & walk
toward me. I smile & wait

for you. The day begins
here. Coffee & tea stands

push back their canvas
covers. A whistle sings

from the train station.
Your arms swing

at your sides like only
a teenage boy's arms

can swing. You look
like you might open

your mouth to sing. There
is no SUV in sight.

I am not sure how
to greet you so I look

at your wet, grass-stained shoes,
then back at your seventeen-

year-old face. I say:
"Come in, out of the rain."

He called Emmett Till a mansion
a mansion of a boy
whose rooms we must fill

Kevin Simmonds
from "The Poet, 1955"

George Zimmerman's Trial

July 13, 2013

Hard to love
a courtroom: jury box silence,

polished wood,
the altitude of judgement.

Hard to love
questions and witnesses'

trembling lips, shivering
memories of rain.

Every courtroom is guilty.
Every testimony

an ache.

Trayvon Martin: Requiem
February 5, 1995 – February 26, 2012

When Words

When words cough
in a hot wind.

When a fist kisses
the concrete over

and over until
bones break, stones

stick to blood
where skin was.

They do not
wash out

and a boy is
gone.

In the Courtroom

In the courtroom
the lawyers used

a foam dummy,
a barely human shape,

faceless and colorless,
just like America

is not.
They hoped

to show the how
and where and if

of a boy's last moments.
To show the how and

and where and if
of a man's worst act.

The lawyers wanted us
to see these questions.

But they failed.
No one can see

questions.

Litany

A mother should
never have to

ask for the body
of her son

more than once.
But in America

this request becomes
a pleading, a litany

to which believers
respond: *No.*

He will not be buried
in Mississippi: *No.*

His name is not John
Doe: *No.*

He was riding
the BART train

home, not starting
anything: *No.*

A collapsed life
should not lie

four hours in a street,
bleeding in protest: *No.*

You may not take
a photograph of

his body: *No.*
His story will not

end in Memphis: *No.*

Rain

Rain does not
bless this

body, like holy
water might. A

boy broken by a
man who was

afraid. A boy
ruined by a

country who is
always afraid.

Rain washes,
like holy water

might. Rain
makes holy,

like holy water
might. But not

this. Some
wounds cannot be

washed clean.
Some sidewalks

will never be holy.
Some nights rain

is a liar. Tonight
rain looks

the same on
living skin

as it does
on dead.

Here

Here are jump shots
that will not

arc toward
anything.

Here are free throws
that will not

silence a gym.
Here are steals

where the point
guard does not see

the ball slapped
away in a blur

of hands and bent
knees. Here,

the guard does not
fall back

on his heels

watching this
boy streak

toward a ghost
basket.

Eight Ways of Looking at the George Zimmerman Trial

1

Every murder is born
somewhere.

This one was born
reaching, like a tree,
one arching branch
bent under
the weight of ashes,
rope, a fruited noose.

2

— *Are you following him?*
— *Yes.*
— *We don't need you to do that.*

3

I pledge allegiance to the flag
of the United States of America
and to the Republic for which it stands.

We stand on ground
when we pledge allegiance.
Allegiance wears a flag.
Flags fly above ground.
Seventeen-year-old boys do not
fly.

4

his candy, your car
him walking, you driving
his parents, your parents
his skin, your gun

5

his

yours

6

He looks like
a crime and the President
at the same time.

7

Some nights when it rains
the cold wraps around
your neck and stumbles
down the center
of your back.

The only prevention,
a hood.

Hoods are sometimes white
and pointed.

Tonight, they are not.

8

We live an impossible
geography. The mapmakers
shake their heads in shame,
unable to ever chart
this landscape:

same country,
different planet.

George Zimmerman's Options

February 26, 2012

Look at the rain from the kitchen window.
Think about staying inside.

Return to the couch in front of the television.
Marvel at Dwayne Wade's perfect follow-through.

Listen to your mother's footsteps upstairs.
Consider taking a ride around the neighborhood.

Consider not.
Back out of the driveway slowly.

Hope there's not a bike on the sidewalk behind you.
Wonder why you didn't check.

Smile to yourself for stopping fully at each stop sign.
Round corners slowly.

Ask yourself why anyone would be walking in this weather.
Notice the pulse of the windshield wipers.

Muse that it sounds peaceful to you.
Watch the hooded person on the sidewalk in the next
block.

Slow down your car.
Feel your annoyance at today's teenagers.

Smile at how foolish that annoyance seems in the rain.
Decide to pull up next to this person.

Pull up next to this person.
Realize he is a teenage boy.

Pull forward as you notice he does not stop walking.
Decide to roll down your window.

Roll down your window.
Look carefully through the rain as he turns to face you.

Decide to ask him if he needs a ride.
Ask.

When Your Word Is a Match

for Willie Louis 1937–2013, who testified
against two men who killed Emmett Till,
1955, Money, Mississippi

When you walk past Klans-
men, smiling at you

on your way into the court
house, wondering how

you will ever live here
after this airless day.

When you tell the story
of a pick-up truck,

a barn, a boy, a threat.
When you point at two

men in the courtroom
and everyone gasps at

what they have never seen
before, but know is true.

When your word is a match-
head, hissing into flame,

testifying aloud but blown
out as soon as you speak.

When all the air
in the courtroom shakes

its white head.
When the smiling men brag

about killing the boy
in the barn. When they

joke about a river, about
what cannot float. When

you flee to the mother's
city, to breathe air that isn't

a gasp. When you hide
the name your parents gave

you for fear the men from
that barn will come

smiling for you too.
When you speak to your wife

years later, after a lifetime
of breathing beside her.

When this air thick as lead
presses your chest to breaking.

When the match's flame
consumes all the air, revealing

a coffin, a boy, a mother,
and you, burning still.

Eighteen Years

for Willie Louis

What in your eighteen years
taught you this language?

Who knew picking cotton
in another man's field

could strengthen your hand
to rise like this?

You heard the lawyer's
question. You knew its

answer, so you raised
your hand from the wooden

witness box and pointed
at two men who knew

nothing of picking cotton,
who knew nothing of

bent backs. You spoke
their names aloud

into air that never knew
yours.

You

for Willie Louis

You didn't know
the boy. He was

no kin to you.
You knew he

was visiting. You
were in ninth

grade. You were
a son too.

You worked in
a field.

Your grandfather knew
your name.

You had been in
the store once.

You had a calendar
that said

1955. You knew
August was

a hot month. You
didn't know

the boy. But you
knew how

to point.

Confederate Flag Dream #1

This small flag
rides on the rear window

of your pick-up truck,
like eyes in the back

of your head, watching
your back, keeping track

of those behind you.
It smiles out your window

like an old man
in need of a friend,

like a young man
who should have lived

a century ago.
This flag will never see

a smooth road,
it wasn't sewn for that.

It will only see night,
baseball bats,

and men beating down
the present,

begging it to be
the past.

Confederate Flag Dream #2

The x on the Confederate flag
is not a cross,

no matter what
Southern Christians say.

Jesus did not create
geometry so they have

no right to claim shapes,
except that of a tree's

arching branch. That shape is one
they own.

The x on this flag is not
a cross. It lies

on its side
and has been pressed down,

misshapen. It is not
a cross even though

blood has spilled
and seeped into it.

The x on the Confederate
flag cannot possibly be

a cross because everyone knows
a cross has flames.

Confederate Flag Dream #3

I wake in the night and dress in darkness.
Black hooded sweatshirt, like a monk
rising for night prayers,
chanting in the language of thieves.

I drive toward a house where a Confederate
flag flies under an American flag
from a pole in the front yard.
I park many yards away so I won't be

seen. Then I walk crouched, hidden,
whispering treason psalms.
I can tell I'm close to the house because
it smells like rope, like a Birmingham church.

I creep toward the flag pole and watch
the house. There is no light. But it breathes
like a sleeping dog, like kerosene.
I lower the flags. The pulleys groan like cowards.

Distant voices scream, crowds laugh,
ropes tighten on straining flesh.
I reach the flag, unhook it and fold its terrors
into my pack. I raise the American flag back up

but only to half-mast.

Requiem for Virgil Ware

Virgil Ware was a 13-year-old boy killed the afternoon of September 15, 1963, just hours after the 16th Street Baptist Church bombing killed four girls in Birmingham, Alabama.

1

The handlebars of a boy's bicycle
can be a crucifixion if the year

is America. If it's your brother's bicycle
and you are laughing like sunshine

on the Docena-Sandusky Road
just outside Birmingham, Alabama. When

you're riding on the handlebars
and your brother, James pedals perfectly,

relying on your laughter to tell
him when to avoid a pothole,

a fallen branch, a red motorcycle he will not
see. The pine and mimosa trees smile

down at you while you dream
about the bike you will make

your own from an uncle's scrap yard.
You'll try to find it there today, piece it

together. Paint it right. Polish its rims.
You'll finally be able to share

a paper route with both your older brothers
and the Ware boys will buy a car,

take girls on dates, go who knows where.
Your eyes are oceans today.

You hum as gravel pops under
the bike tires. You smile loud as

the wind singing past your ears.
That wind, the only breath you need

on this Sunday afternoon.

2

Larry Joe Sims was a sixteen year-old
boy you did not know. He had just

bought a small Confederate flag at a rally.
He knew there'd been a bomb at a church

that morning. He knew there was a cross
atop that church. He heard some Negro

boys were throwing rocks. His
friend, Michael, drove a motorcycle

red as Alabama air. Larry clung to the back.
Michael boasted about a pearl-

handled revolver. Larry hadn't
believed him. Michael handed it

to Larry as they sped along the
Docena-Sandusky Road. Larry

held the revolver reverently. He
had fired a gun before. His eyes were

fine. His vision clear. He could see
the road before them.

3

There is nothing so beautiful
as a boy's sweat. When you are thirteen

years old and you can't control your smile.
When you dream of your own bike.

When you see it in your mind and
imagine its candy apple red

or forest green frame, you're not sure which.
That joy paints the world. That joy sweats.

Your older brother, James pedals fierce.
His warm breath brushes your neck.

You love your brother's breath.
You knows its smell. Its taste.

You hope your brother will breathe forever.

4

You didn't know a brick church
shivered this morning. You

didn't know the face of Christ
shattered out of its famous stained-

glass window. You didn't know
the basement filled with bricks falling

from the sanctuary above it.
You didn't know that four girls

were carried out, you never knew
silence so hot.

But even if you'd known, you
might have pushed the thought

aside. The rising joy of your own
bike would smile everything else

away. Its joy is that bright. Its
sweat is that perfect.

5

The red paint on Michael's motorcycle
is almost as dark as the red

on Larry's small Confederate flag
snapping in the Sabbath wind.

It makes him believe something
he can not name. He leans

into his friend's back and holds
the revolver in his left hand.

He thinks about the new school year at
Phillips High School. He is an Eagle

Scout. He sometimes prays to the one
who died on a cross. He is an

American. He knows his family
thinks some civil rights

are a good idea but it will still
be funny to scare these two

Black boys on a bike. He'll
laugh when their eyes open

with fear, seeing the gun.
He expects them to throw

rocks but they don't.
He plans to fire the gun at the ground

and then laugh hard as sunshine.
He knows he shouldn't close

his eyes when firing a gun
but he does anyway. He does

not see the bullets hit Virgil's
chest and cheek. He does not

hear Virgil's breath pull in fast.
He laughs down the road on the back

of Michael's motorcycle. He does not see
them pull over and fall because

he closed his eyes.

6

You were smart and skinny.
You had faith that your brother would

keep the bike up. You knew you could
wrap your arms around the handlebars

and not fall. You believed in balance,
your toes on the front wheel's bolts.

You would not fall. You played tight end
in football, you knew how to extend

your arms. You knew how to rise.

7

Until this afternoon turned dark. Until
you heard laughter like mocking

soldiers. Until you lay on your back
beside the road, James above you

begging you to stop trembling. Until
air became hard in your throat. Until

the pines loomed over you, piercing
the red Alabama sky like nails.

Until you never saw your brother, James
so scared. Until you needed your

brother's breath for yourself now.
Until you wanted these crucified seconds:

his face, his sweat, his breath
to last forever.

Requiem for Johnny Robinson

*Johnny Robinson was a 16-year-old boy killed by a Birmingham,
Alabama police officer September 15, 1963, just hours after the 16th
Street Baptist Church bombing.*

1

You cannot play a game of catch
with your country

if your country is 1963
and people smile when they say

Bombingham, Alabama. You
cannot stand at a gas station

after a church has been bombed
unless you want to ignite

a year of flames. You cannot be
sixteen years old, a boy, and Black

without knowing there is always
a gun in the back window

of a police car. There is always
a man holding that gun

with his finger on your back.
You already know

you cannot play catch with him.
You already know a stone

is not a bullet.

2

But when you're sixteen and a car
draped in the Confederate flag cruises

by on the same day a church fell
onto four little girls, you can be

excused for not remembering
that gas stations burn like a country,

that a shotgun has a fuse too.

3

Jack Parker had been a police officer
for twelve years when he saw

you from behind, your legs running. He
sat in the police car's back seat

with a shotgun pointing at your
future. A gun like this is made

by men. It does not grow in nature.
It does not remember anyone's name.

It does not sing. It is not used to play
catch. The police car blocked one

end of the alley so you and your friends
ran to the other end. All he knew

was that you and your friends looked
like the kind who throw stones at cars.

Maybe the police car jerked forward
and he squeezed the trigger without

meaning it, some said. Maybe
the driver hit the brakes too hard,

some said. Maybe an all-white
police department has a word

for this. Jack Parker would sign
a newspaper advertisement opposing

the integration of the Birmingham
Police Department, just days after

shooting you in the back. He might
have played catch with his children

later that day.

4

You had called your sister
asking her to bring a plate

of food to the gas station. It was Sunday,
after all, and you and your friends were

standing at the station on 26th Street.
You'd heard other teenagers were shouting

from cars with Confederate flags. You'd
seen the church, the smoke. You'd tasted

the silence when four ambulances
drove up. Your sister brought you dinner

and then dropped the plate to run
toward the hospital when she heard
you'd been kissed on the back

by your country.
You had six hours to live. You

spent them on your stomach.

5

Your mother had four words
as she pounded her fists on

an officer's chest at the hospital:
"You killed my son." She raged.

Her pieta was complete. She
began losing words. She only

had three when she saw your sister
running breathless into the hospital:

"Your brother dead," she said,
more times than anyone can

remember. A trinity of words that
can save no one. No one prays

to a god by that name. You
had a tag tied to your foot. The tag

had a number on it. Your mother
never knew what it was.

No one plays catch with their country.

That's the Sound of the Men Working on the Chain Gang

After Sam Cooke — Thanks to Terrance Hayes

There wasn't an orange jumpsuit small enough
for the shoulders he woke up with this morning.
But determined to breathe like the man

his sixteen-year-old mind told him he was,
he took the Department of Corrections suit
marked "small" off the hook and stepped into it

quickly, pulling up the suicide-proof plastic zipper
with teenage energy. He could almost hide
in the spill of this suit today while he

and the others were allowed to go out and collect
the free world's trash from beside the Beltway.
He could wear this orange scream of an outfit

that made him look like an emergency.
He could work beside their van and its trailer
carrying a Port-a-Potty, near the guards whose

caffeinated fingers rested on their guns, their gaze
never slipping far from his and the other prisoners'
orange-wrapped legs. Maybe he could hum as he breathed

all that free-world air racing past him at seventy-five
miles an hour. Maybe he could even sing a little,
imagining he was riding in one of those SUVs with a

booming radio, or a red convertible with the whipping
air stealing his melody as quickly as he sings it,
hurling his voice into the lanes of flying traffic.

He could pull all that Sunday-air deep into his lungs
and imagine he is a thousand courtrooms away
from the side of this road, singing a song no one else

can hear, a song that does not end
with the slamming steel of a cell door.

Mohamed Bouazizi Pushed a Wheelbarrow

Tunis, December 17, 2010

Mohamed Bouazizi pushed
a wheelbarrow heaped with red onions
and figs. One wheel round as hope,

figs sweet as his wife. A policeman's voice
said he did not have a vendor's permit
so the policeman's leather boot flipped

his wheelbarrow, scattering onions
onto the street where a dog sniffed
them, figs rolled to the wet curb.

The wheel turned in the angry air.
Mohamed saw this with his eyes,
so he complained with his hands,

upturned in the universal language
of pleading, reminding the officers he has
sold produce on this corner for years.

They mocked him, arguing
like unfed crows. Finally, one officer slapped
his face and spat at him, taking

his electronic scales and flipping
over his wheelbarrow, yet again.
Mohamed's eyes took on the color of shame,

his sweat smelled like shadows.
To counter the darkness, he bought gasoline
and a match and poured the gasoline over

himself, lighting his country afire.
Eighteen days later, after a hospital visit
from the country's president, Mohamed

Bouazizi died, his ashes clinging to all skin
that is human: shrouding, reminding us
that Mohamed Bouazizi pushed a wheelbarrow.

There must be nothing
there but appetite.

Kyle Dargan
from "How to Lick a Blade"

On "The Resurrection of Lazarus"
by Henry O. Tanner

He stood still, calmly
looking down at you.

But bedlam frenzied
everywhere else.

Riot wrestled belief.
Martha covered her face

with living hands.
Mary gazed stricken into

everything that breathed.
Some stared at you

in panic, others praised
the God, whose heart

you must have
torn.

On "The Annunciation"
by Henry O. Tanner

Mary sat on the edge
of the bed, sleeplessness

her only lover. She waited,
draped in morning, hunched

under the weight of questions:
"How can this be?" visible

through her transparent skin.
"I do not know" wells up

in her eyes, waiting. Her
hands grasp one another

to still the trembling always
found near a cross.

She thought you came
a few days ago but she

busied herself, not wanting
any part of this calvary.

She had no magnificat
to sing, no "Be it done to

me" in her breath yet.
Still, she stares now, her eyes

fixed, not on faith, but on
a light she can barely believe

is light.

On "Nicodemus"
by Henry O. Tanner

He sat anxious, hands
clutching his knees,

leaning forward for fear
he would be caught.

But his night-colored robes
knew he already was.

He listened in dread of hearing
his own name. He saw his own

days in the words you whispered.
He asked questions he knew

the answers to. He thought prophet
but hoped messiah.

He stared at your hands, wondering
how long they would be whole.

He tasted broken bread
without knowing why.

On "The Pilgrims of Emmaus"
by Henry O. Tanner

Some meals come true
in a second. Their truth lives

before you and then it is gone,
but not gone. You want

to reach across the table
to touch the food that looks

like light. You want to beg
it to stay always. This table

took the shape of your fear.
Now it feels like a cross

the size of your hope.
Everything you knew

slipped away, fading
into shadow, disappearing

into a crumb of bread.

On Jean-Michel Basquiat's "Riding with Death"

When these bones prance
and clatter, we taste a grace,

a water path, carrying us to thirst.
These bones know the way.

They have traveled this
earthen road, they have

worn its smell though
today their whiteness is

naked as air. We ride
on bones all our lives.

We balance without using
our hands, no need to hold

on to anything. Falling is not
falling. We hold out our arms

like the crucified: almost
bone, some skin, mostly

illusion. We ride with death
true as dirt,

but we believe we are
walking on our own

two feet.

On Jean-Michel Basquiat's "Horn Players"

A triptych is made for praise. Where
two or three are gathered, there

is a choir, a jazz trio staring out,
from a painting, at the thirsty world,

offering its life-blood, its spit,
blessed into a saxophone's bowl.

The monk's begging bowl, now
its chalice, the place where praise

can be born. Here, Gillespie prays
from the left. His golden eyes

meditate on the horn he holds
to his chest. He is battered

by words from every sacred
text yet he sings none of them.

Parker prays from the right,
a shadow of sparrows taking

flight all at once, they rise like
fog, mixing spit and air hoping

to make gold, the alchemist's joke:
everyone knows teeth can't

fly. Everyone knows soap
can't clean the artist's wounds.

Everyone knows a word crossed
out is still a word.

The center panel must be
where you pray, in the language

of stroke and hue. You color
each prayer, you turn your cheek,

your face shredded with tears
too warm for this world.

On Jean-Michel Basquiat's "Red Kings"

You are crowned
in silence. The lament

of stillness. Your mouth,
the finest vowel.

Your name almost
emerges and then recedes,

a memory we can't
quite tamp down or see

clearly. You are old. Maybe
a door. Maybe a window

pane no longer lit
from within. You are

golden thorns. You look
past us, nervous.

You sit beside
your oldest friend. He

has no name but he is
crowned too. He looks

straight through us.
He knows you are there.

His teeth, a permanent
orchestra tuning up,

playing one note, its
octaves, straining, tight,

ready and anxious to bleed.

To Jean-Michel Basquiat: SAMO

*SAMO was Basquiat's graffiti tag referring
to "mindwash religion, nowhere politics,
and bogus philosophy."*

You were born
so you could die.

You were the well-
walked road. The mis-

take we kiss.
The scab we caress.

The wound on
repeat. A video loop

of lies we drink
as a gospel.

Then you proved
your shadow truth.

You predicted your-
self: The artist dies

young, the cliché
lives forever.

Our anger is a kiss
too. Fury sometimes

a scab. Is this all
you could do?

No blank canvas
left? No old door lying

under a brown man
riding with death?

There was the method of kneeling,
a fine method, if you lived in a country
where stones were smooth.

Naomi Shihab Nye
from "Different Ways to Pray"

Praise Song / Sorrow Song: REEFA

---

for Israel Hernandez, an 18 year-old graffiti artist,
tased to death by police in Miami Beach on August 6, 2013.
His graffiti tag was REEFA.

Praise to the letter "R"
you had just begun to paint.

Praise to the stream of black,
forceful and skinny as you.

Praise to the corner of 71st & Collins,
the wall of an abandoned McDonald's.

Praise to August 6th,
a Miami night holding its breath.

Praise to the shoes of the police
as they approached you.

Praise to their badges,
bright with shame.

Praise to all seven of them
who chased you.

Praise to running.

Praise to the fearful heaving
in your chest.

Praise to a different
heaving in theirs.

Praise to the white iron fence
you jumped.

Praise to the wall on Harding Avenue
where they cornered you.

Praise to their laughter
at you cornered.

Praise to the officer
who remembered his taser.

Praise to remembering.

Praise to the piercing
as it entered your chest.

Praise to your chest,
all 147 pounds of you.

Praise to the darkness
you saw closing your eyes.

Praise to closing.

Praise to the pavement
that caught you.

Praise to the high-fives the officers
slapped afterward.

Praise to Vista Memorial for
donating your funeral and burial.

Praise to burial.

Sorrow to your skateboard,
silent and still.

Sorrow to your backpack
that probably slowed you down.

Sorrow to the wooden casket, polished,
waiting to be tagged.

Sorrow to your name,
not painted there.

Sorrow to the attorney who said,
"Our hearts go out to his family."

Sorrow to hearts gone out.

Sorrow to the letter "R" you did not
finish.

Sorrow to finishing.

Praise Song / Sorrow Song: DEMZ

*for Delbert Gutierrez, a 21-year-old Miami graffiti artist
who died on December 9, 2014, after being struck by a police car.
His graffiti tag was DEMZ.*

Praise to a warm December night,
stars and palm trees dreaming.

Praise to the words you
dreamed of painting.

Praise to the gravel beneath
the unmarked police car.

Praise to you running, your
quick moves through the alley.

Praise to alleys.

Praise to the police car's tires
hissing around corners.

Praise to the dark clothing
you wore that night.

Praise to your shock as the front bumper
tore your legs.

Praise to the surprise at being
struck by so much weight.

Praise to collapsing, your arms'
and legs' betrayal.

Praise to betrayal.

Praise to the metal and pavement
as they open your head.

Praise to the darkness that leaks
from your eyes.

Praise to your eyes.

Sorrow to the night your mother grieved
beside your hospital bed.

Sorrow to not knowing
she was there.

Sorrow to her fingers laced
through yours.

Sorrow to the police official who told her
you shouldn't have run.

Sorrow for the dinner he offered
to buy her.

Sorrow for her fury.

Sorrow for all the December nights
you survived.

Sorrow that this one
was different.

For the Graffiti Artist Whose Tag Covered the Last Cool "Disco" Dan Tag in Washington, D.C.

I'd like to believe
you didn't know.

Your white paint pen
got full of itself and you

let it swagger unsupervised.
You didn't know how

long or how gently
Cool "Disco" Dan's name

has starved across
our city, has smiled

just around the corner
of that brick garage,

train car, liquor store.
I'd like to believe you

are young and that your
youth grins like an excuse.

But it's hard to see
a tombstone defaced.

It's hard to watch a
newcomer ignore a friend.

I'd like to believe everyone
deserves forgiveness.

But some wounds
last. Some histories need

to be rewritten.

On Langston Hughes'
"The Negro Speaks of Rivers"

You wrote of rivers
that deepened you,

of water doing what it does
to earth, to us,

cutting down and rinsing
away anything that is not tomorrow.

Today those rivers cut still:
Mothers bury their sons

in the sand of the Euphrates
as the sun sinks

below a barbed wire horizon.
The huts clustered along

the Congo are filled
with human limbs,

no eyes, no faces,
and the married fingers have

been stripped of their rings.
The Nile too still flows,

admiring the monuments
of staring stone

but along its banks
crouch madmen, dipping

their missing fingers into its
moving water.

And the only song rising
from the Mississippi

emerges from a woman left
on her roof, shaking her fist

as the hurricane laughs,
the waters rise, while some

in her own country
pretend she is dancing.

There is only one thing
to know here:

we are meaner than deep,
we forgive less than we

harm. We are silent
in the face of almost

everything.

On Langston Hughes' "Theme for English B"

In Memory of Kevin Nelson, 1985-2004

When I told my creative writing
class of high school seniors

to let a "a page come out"
of them, to write something

"true," they looked at me
like I was slow.

"Write something true?"
Hythia said, in her Pontius Pilate

accent. "What is True?"
"Well," I explained,

"sit with that idea
for a minute and see

what comes." It wasn't
the first time my prompt

for in-class writing
stumbled and fell to the floor

between my black students
and me, their white

poetry teacher. But it was
a first, a few days later,

when our discussion led Kevin
to say, "Maybe everything is true."

What Can Be Said

for Miles

What can be said
of the white cop

who spat on my Black
student in the 2am

silence beside Hwy 270?
Did the vigilant oaks

slip steel into your
blood? Did you think

the stars could not see
in the dark? Did you

imagine darkness has
no conscience, would

not speak up?

And what of my student,
this young man

lying on the ground
behind a car, trembling

amid the 2am choir of
seizure and panic?

That his shivering
asthma scared you so

much you couldn't breathe?
Bitch the only word

to dance off your tongue?
Spit the only language

you could speak?

For Z Who Lost His Mother in Hurricane Katrina

September, 2005

He had a vague memory
of what it meant to breathe,

but here, he had to diligently
re-learn so many lessons.

Friends slapped him on the back
in welcome, but they were not

friends just yet.
Teachers sighed when they saw him

as one more student
in an already flooded class.

When he gazed at himself
in the mirror, he squinted,

trying to recognize the face
of this young man who appeared

to be alive in all the normal ways,
but who had learned to live

without air.

and on the front page
of the newspapers, the corpses

Niki Herd
from "And on the Front Page"

Immigrants

No one loves
a border.

Closed roses,
an open fist.

We live on one
side or the other

of every ache.

Santo Toribio: Sweatshirt

St. Toribio Romo Gonzalez, 1900-1928, a Mexican priest said to guide immigrants in need who pray to him. Immigrants are known to pin his picture inside their clothing as protection.

Your wrinkled image
secured inside

his sweatshirt, safety-
pinned on four

sides so he feels you
press his own

sweating skin.
You, a serious saint:

lips that say prayers,
eyes that mean martyrdom.

Your stories are legend
among the near-dead.

That they dreamed of you
and woke to water.

That they prayed to you
and found apples

in the desert. That
they gazed at your image

and heard your warning
to go back, later

to learn there was more
desert than they

could breathe. Your hands
anointed for wandering

souls. Your hands tilting
the chalice to the lips

of a starving faith.

Santo Toribio: Water Litany

For tongues gone grey
as greed. *Pray for us.*

For mothers dropping
the last wet diamonds

onto lips of ash.
Pray for us.

For throats where even
the blood has dried.

Pray for us.
For amber eyes that see

a shimmering which
is a whole country

laughing. *Pray for us.*
For the ache that is

an underground river.
Pray for us. For the oasis

dream that comes
too easily to the scared.

Pray for us,
who have no country,

no air, only a river,
a fence, and you.

Santo Toribio: Chapel

The desert wind whispers
through ocotillo branches,

shredded fingers pleading
to a silent sky.

They say when we are
close to death we will

see you, hear you, words
of comfort, maybe a jar

of water, maybe your hand
will point to the true north.

We stopped at your chapel
in Jalisco but felt no comfort

there. We had too many miles
ahead of us, too many countries.

We saw your image in the
stained glass window, holding

a canteen and a cup. But we
need the miracle, not the mirage.

Santo Toribio: Altar

You too died in the middle
of the night.

Soldiers woke you
with cursing guns.

Your sister saw you shot,
the floor became an altar.

You lived in a country
where saints were

illegal, where breaking
bread sounded like

gunfire. Although you never
heard the desert,

did not leave your country,
we carry you, sewn

inside our coats, our
paper saint, the martyr

we hope will save us
when we lie torn

beneath the cactus,
on an altar of sand.

March 24, 1980

for Archbishop Óscar Romero of El Salvador

The cup you raised
was round, not unlike

a bullet. It widened
like a wound does. It held

the swirling of the people
but it could not contain

it. The cup held a wine not
served at fine meals. This

wine knew garbage dumps,
El Mozote, Santiago de Maria,

places no bishop would ever see.
You took the poor into

your arms, encircling them
with a cathedral's protection,

radio sermons to help them
bury the ones who died

before you would.
One day ago, you ordered

soldiers to see their country,
to disobey any who ordered

them to close their eyes and
kill their own. "Stop" you

demanded, the swelling circle
of a bleeding land.

And so today in a hospital
chapel, a few nuns, tired

nurses who'd read
the treasonous gospel.

The story of a cathedral
unfinished as its people.

The story of a bishop
firm as his altar.

The story of a cup
dangerous as its last

supper, a banquet
of bullets for the Savior's

country to taste.

If a Joshua Tree Is Made

If a Joshua Tree is made
of stone, its lips must be

plump and moist like
the desert, its dangerous lover.

But if a Joshua Tree is
made of flesh, then

its lips are knives,
shining, lying, bare—

still dangerous, still shading
every dream God could dream.

Beneath this tree a woman
calms a curious child, a man

worries whose lips to believe,
whose knives to trust.

Eventually, every immigrant
learns this hourly truth:

No desert tree can be
trusted, every root holds

the potential for starvation,
the possibility of brilliant

suffering.

Joshua Trees Grow

Joshua Trees grow
in the language of begging,

their wicked fingers scratch
at the indifferent face of God.

They rake the skin and draw
blood, but the blood looks

like hiding, like
God's brown face.

And God does not smile
at any of this.

He grimaces in the language
of cracked lips, of tongues

copper and scared.

At Night Joshua Trees Exhale

At night, Joshua Trees exhale
a heavy breath.

It tastes like running
in the dark. Its branches seem to

widen out of respect for
the frightened shadows

only this tree can see.
Joshua Trees empty themselves

in one warm breath, hoping
the sky, their bleeding lover,

will protect them from
the fists and flashing lights

whose uniforms blind,
whose nightstick beams invade

the crouching life
under every breathing tree:

a wanderer, a swimmer
in sand, relieved

that a gasp is almost silent.

No Child Climbs a Joshua Tree

No child climbs a Joshua Tree,
no tree houses ever perch

in these branches. No pirate
searches for land from these

bristling limbs. Only the occasional
ghost of a refugee cuddles

and sleeps among its spines;
its thorns, a blanket protecting

every immigrant from this
illegal country.

If You Leave Your Shoes

If you leave your shoes
on the front porch
when you run

to the city pool
for swimming lessons,
you might end up

walking across the sand
of the desert in
scorched feet,

bare, like the prophets,
who knew what it was
to burn.

If you leave your lover
to run to the market
for bread and pears

you might return
to find your lover
gone and the bed

covered with knives,
hot and gleaming from
a morning in the sun.

If you leave your country
in the wrong hands,
you might return to

see it drowning in blood,
able to spit
but not to speak.

For Gilberto Ramos

15-year-old Guatemalan boy who died
in the Texas desert, June, 2014

Before you left, your mother
draped you with fifty Hail Marys,

a rosary of white wood,
a constellation she hoped might

guide you. But Texas does not
know these prayers. It knows

that desert air is thirsty
and you are made of water.

It drank you slowly. Your name
only linked to your body by the string

of Aves still around your neck,
the small cross pressing against your

wooden skin, the color of another cross.
You left home on May seventeenth

with one change of clothes and two
countries ahead of you, your brother's

phone number hidden on the back
of your belt buckle so the coyote

couldn't find it. The coyotes pray
in the language of extortion.

The phone number was found
by a Texas official whose name

your brother couldn't remember. She called
and spoke in the language of bones. He translated

her news into "pray for us, sinners,
now and at the hour of our death."

His prayer meant "brother," a word
he kept moist, just beneath his tongue.

Acknowledgments

I am grateful to the editors of these journals and websites who published the following poems, sometimes in slightly different versions:

Assaracus: "Meeting"

Wordpeace: "Trayvon Martin: Requiem"

Valley Voices: "George Zimmerman's Options" "Praise Song/Sorrow Song: REEFA"

Poet Lore: "When Your Word Is a Match" "Eighteen Years" "Confederate Flag Dream #2"

Tidal Basin Review: "That's the Sound of the Men Working on the Chain Gang" "On Langston Hughes' 'The Negro Speaks of Rivers'"

Little Patuxent Review: "On 'The Annunciation' by Henry O. Tanner"

Origins Journal: "Praise Song/Sorrow Song: DEMZ" "March 24, 1980"

Truck Blog: "What Can Be Said"

Fledgling Rag: "If a Joshua Tree Is Made" "Joshua Trees Grow" "At Night Joshua Trees Exhale" "No Child Climbs a Joshua Tree"

Poetry of Resistance: Voices of Social Justice: "If You Leave Your Shoes"

The Los Angeles Times: "For Gilberto Ramos"

Song for a Passbook Torch: A Nelson Mandela Poetry Anthology: "Nelson Mandela Speaks to Hector Pieterson" "Nelson Mandela Speaks to Trayvon Martin"

Gratitude

I am filled with gratitude for Bryan Borland and Seth Pennington of Sibling Rivalry Press. Their passion for these poems is only matched by mine. Thanks to Fred Joiner for introducing me to the surprising joys of jazz, especially the music of John Coltrane. Thanks to my colleague and friend Helen Free for pointing me in the direction of Henry O. Tanner. Thanks to Jefferson Pinder for suggesting a night raid to take down and steal a Confederate flag. Thanks to the anonymous graffiti artist who introduced me to DEMZ and REEFA. Thanks to poets and friends Francisco X. Alarcon, Stevi Calandra, Carmen Calatayud, Nahshon Cook, Kyle Dargan, Hayes Davis, Odilia Galvan Rodriguez, Le Hinton, Randall Horton, Lang Kanai, Alan King, Steven Leyva, Orlando Pinder, Katy Richey, Maritza Rivera, Miles Taylor, Truth Thomas, and Venus Thrash. Thanks to my colleagues and students at Gonzaga College High School for their encouragement. Thanks to Sarah Browning, Martín Espada, and Afaa Michael Weaver. As always, thanks to Robert for listening, fixing, and caring.

About the Poet

Joseph Ross' first two collections of poetry, *Gospel of Dust* (2013) and *Meeting Bone Man* (2012) were published by Main Street Rag Publishing. His poems appear in many publications and anthologies including *The Los Angeles Times, Poet Lore, Tidal Basin Review, Beltway Poetry Quarterly,* and *Drumvoices Revue.* He has received multiple Pushcart Prize nominations and won the 2012 Pratt Library / *Little Patuxent Review* Poetry Prize. He recently served as the 23rd Poet-in-Residence for the Howard County Poetry and Literature Society in Howard County, Maryland. He teaches English and Creative Writing at Gonzaga College High School in Washington, D.C., and writes regularly at www.josephross.net.

About the Press

Sibling Rivalry Press is an independent press based in Little Rock, Arkansas. It is a sponsored project of Fractured Atlas, a nonprofit arts service organization. Contributions to support the operations of Sibling Rivalry Press are tax-deductible to the extent permitted by law, and your donations will directly assist in the publication of work that disturbs and enraptures. To contribute to the publication of more books like this one, please visit our website and click *donate*.

Sibling Rivalry Press gratefully acknowledges the following donors, without whom this book would not be possible:

TJ Acena	JP Howard	Tina Parker
Kaveh Akbar	Shane Khosropour	Brody Parrish Craig
John-Michael Albert	Randy Kitchens	Patrick Pink
Kazim Ali	Jørgen Lien	Dennis Rhodes
Seth Eli Barlow	Stein Ove Lien	Paul Romero
Virginia Bell	Sandy Longhorn	Robert Siek
Ellie Black	Ed Madden	Scott Siler
Laure-Anne Bosselaar	Jessica Manack	Alana Smoot Samuelson
Dustin Brookshire	Sam & Mark Manivong	Loria Taylor
Alessandro Brusa	Thomas March	Hugh Tipping
Jessie Carty	Telly McGaha & Justin Brown	Alex J. Tunney
Philip F. Clark	Donnelle McGee	Ray Warman & Dan Kiser
Morell E. Mullins	David Meischen	Ben Westlie
Jonathan Forrest	Ron Mohring	Valerie Wetlaufer
Hal Gonzales	Laura Mullen	Nicholas Wong
Diane Greene	Eric Nguyen	Anonymous (18)
Brock Guthrie	David A. Nilsen	
Chris Herrmann	Joseph Osmundson	

www.ingramcontent.com/pod-product-compliance
Lightning Source LLC
Chambersburg PA
CBHW031141090426
42738CB00008B/1178